THE
MOST INCREDIBLE
YouTube
VIDEOS EVER!

First published in Great Britain in 2015 by Prion Books

an imprint of the
Carlton Publishing Group
20 Mortimer Street
London W1T 3JW

A CIP catalogue for this book is available
from the British Library.

ISBN 978-1-85375-929-1

Printed and bound by CPI Group (UK) Ltd, Croydon CR0 4YY

10 9 8 7 6 5 4 3 2 1

THE
MOST INCREDIBLE
YouTube
VIDEOS EVER!

Your guide to the coolest, craziest and funniest internet clips

PRION

I'm sure if Shakespeare were alive today, he'd be
doing classic guitar solos on YouTube.

Peter Capaldi

INTRODUCTION

Despite celebrating its tenth birthday in February 2015, YouTube continues to be the world's favourite internet site. With 300 hours of video are uploaded every minute, there is something to suit every interest. Music, comedy, cats and dogs remain incredibly popular, but many just love the never-ending supply of weird, hilarious, jaw-dropping, surreal and completely awesome clips. It's no wonder there are a billion individual users visiting each month!

The selection in this book points you towards the videos that have made the news, gone super-viral or which are so good that people just return again and again to view them. You can see recent hits such as the Mutant Giant Spider Dog, the Sia Chandelier Parody, the Devil Baby Attack and the Zombie Rooftop Chase as well as YouTube favourites, including Honest Movie Trailers, Bad Lip Reading, The Slo-Mo Guys and People Are Awesome. And, of course, there are hilarious funnies, epic pranks, musical mash-ups, cute pets and loads, loads more.

INAPPROPRIATE LANGUAGE WARNING

The videos selected in this book do not contain any scenes of an explicit sexual or extremely gross nature. However, there is the occasional use of bad language, which is sometimes part of the video's humour. The comments sections of many of the clips often contain unnecessarily offensive, puerile and abusive language. They rarely feature any remarks of value and are generally worth switching off or ignoring.

DON'T TRY THIS AT HOME

Some of the book's clips feature stunts performed either by professionals or under the supervision of professionals. Accordingly the publishers must insist that no one attempt to re-create or re-enact any stunt or activity performed on the featured videos.

HOW TO VIEW THE CLIPS

Each entry is accompanied by a QR code, which you can scan with your iPad or iPod. Alternatively, there is a short URL address, which you can type into your own computer, tablet or phone. Unfortunately, many of the clips are preceded by adverts, which can often be skipped after a few seconds or you may wish to download a reputable advert blocker to prevent them appearing.

CONTENTS

I go on YouTube when somebody
says to look something up.

George Clooney

MUTANT GIANT SPIDER DOG

**Mayhem on the streets as the spider
dog goes on the rampage**

It looks real enough. And terrifying enough. A giant mutant spider is roaming the streets, chasing its victims into the enormous webs it has built. But this is the brilliant work of Polish YouTuber Sylwester Wardega. He has dressed his dog Chica in a spider costume, let him loose in the local streets, and filmed the ensuing mayhem. People going about their lives are naturally scared out of their wits and even more frightened as they come across the rope webs that Sylwester has rigged up, complete with fake human remains. His reward for such imagination was to earn the Number 1 "top trending video" of 2014.

http://y2u.be/YoB8t0B4jx4

ANACONDA DANCE TRIUMPH

11-year-old dancer wins the internet with her dance interpretation

Nicki Minaj might have wowed them with the raunchy video to her song 'Anaconda', but an 11-year-old girl won the internet with her pure dance interpretation of the song. Taylor and her choreographer, Laurence Kaiwai, were filmed dancing along to the hit track at Edmonton's KORE dance studio. The studio crowd seem to enjoy it, but as soon as it was uploaded to YouTube it went viral. Millions agreed that Taylor had nailed it and her star kept rising. She was invited on the *Ellen DeGeneres Show* and continued to upload amazing dances.

http://y2u.be/pIZphVSrR-0

RESCUE CAT

The hero cat that sees off a vicious dog

All that his parents knew was that their four-year-old son had been attacked by a dog. It wasn't until they viewed the security camera footage that the whole extraordinary story emerged. Little Jeremy Triantafilo was pedalling his tricycle around the front yard when he was pounced on by a vicious neighbour's dog that had escaped its leash. Suddenly, out of nowhere, a flash of black appears, bundles the dog off the boy and then chases the hound away. That flash was none other than Tara, the family cat. "The cat saved me," Jeremy told a local paper. " My kitty's a hero."

http://y2u.be/LSG_wBiTEE8S

A HAPPY SWIFTMAS TO ALL

**The remarkable Taylor Swift makes Christmas special
for fans with personalized presents**

A near tidal wave threatened America at Christmas 2014 when
hundreds of teenage girls cried gallons of tears after receiving
presents from singer Taylor Swift. Cynicism aside, this video
documents the pop star's unprecedented acts of kindness,
which she refers to as "Swiftmas". It shows Taylor wrapping up
personalised presents for selected fans, and gifts being opened
with squealing gratitude. In one case Taylor even drives miles to
personally deliver presents to a fan and her son. Many celebrities
repeat how much their fans mean to them, but few give this kind
of time and effort to making them feel special.

http://y2u.be/j3yyF31jbKo

THE MID-AIR *CIRCLE OF LIFE*

A cappella on the airways with the cast of *The Lion King*

You've just fastened your seatbelt, checked your phone is switched off, kicked off your shoes and sat back ready for your flight. What you least expect is to be given a private performance by the professional cast of *The Lion King*. That's exactly what happened to passengers on Flight 097 from Brisbane to Sydney, who were treated to a full-scale rendition of 'The Circle of Life'. In fine voice, the performers from *The Lion King* Australia go full throttle with a capella harmonies and handclaps galore. It certainly beats sitting next to the screaming child.

http://y2u.be/wgSLxl1oAwA

MEAT THE NEIGHBOURS

A prankster is out looking for trouble – or is he?

"You want beef?" Maybe it's not as common a phrase in Britain
as in the States, but we get the idea. It means "You want to
make something of it?" or "You want to fight me?" BigDawsTv, a
YouTube prankster, went around his local streets asking people
if they wanted beef and it's surprising how many were willing
to take him up on it. Perhaps equally surprising is how many of
them were willing to see the funny side when he revealed the
ground beef he'd taped to the inside of his shirt.

http://y2u.be/tfZa1l8lxDo

PRICKLY EATER

The YouTube eating hero takes on his daftest challenge yet

Of course, he doesn't eat a cactus. No. He eats *two* cacti! The LA Beast (real name, Kevin Strahle) has form for this kind of thing. He is a professional competitive eater with a seemingly masochistic passion for the most excruciating challenges. They include eating 36 eggs (with the shell), drinking a gallon of Tabasco hot sauce and shaving his beard with wax strips. But none come close to the pain of the cactus. There is also a video of the aftermath if you like to see a man suffer.

http://y2u.be/d4KPWOUkbw8

ICE BUCKET CHALLENGED

The best and funniest fails from the great Ice Bucket Challenge

The Ice Bucket Challenge was all over 2014, and anyone with a camera filmed themselves being doused with freezing cold water in aid of the ALS charity. Even the great and good were persuaded to join in. Search for "Celebrities ALS Ice Bucket Challenge" and you'll find everyone from Miley Cyrus to Selena Gomez to David Beckham getting a cold soaking for charity. This video is far funnier, though: the Ice Bucket fails. A whole lot can go wrong when idiots, buckets and water come together and the great thing about the challenge is that there is always a camera running!

http://y2u.be/uCromp-kIUU

THE CAT THAT GOT THE CREAM — AND STILL SCOWLS

Here is Grumpy Cat — she's not really grumpy and that isn't her real name

---

Her real name is Tadar Sauce, but everyone calls her Grumpy Cat and she is the most famous real live cat in the world. Grumpy Cat was only six months old in September 2012 when her photos first went viral online. Now she has a million Facebook friends, 30 million views on her YouTube videos and is soon to star in her own blockbuster film. So what's she got to be grumpy about? Poor Tadar was just born with a grumpy face, a loveable grumpy face that now adorns t-shirts and Christmas cards.

http://y2u.be/INscMGmhmX4

THE DOG TEASER

Magician uses disappearing dog treats as the ultimate dog tease

We've all had fun teasing our four-legged friends, even if it's just pretending to throw a stick and watching them scurry off towards the horizon. Magician Jose Ahonen is a dog teaser in a class of his own. He offers them a dog treat under their very noses, but before they get a chance to snap it up, he makes it vanish. The dogs' reactions are priceless. Desperately looking around, even nature's own detectives are bemused and befuddled by a sleight of hand. Dog lovers can rest easy: we are assured that all participants were soon rewarded with enough treats to compensate.

http://y2u.be/VEQXeLjY9ak

A CORPORATE VIDEO THAT ISN'T DULL!

A clever and hilarious parody of business jargon and corporate nonsense

---

This is a real advert for a real company and it's a piece of genius. IT company Risual have ripped the corporate video apart and put it back in a hilarious way. Despite claiming to have a "S**t ton of clients" and to be "the winners of every award for everything ever", the company still throws the kitchen sink at the ad in a brilliant parody of business speak and aspirational jargon. They cleverly subvert the IT stereotype and in the final logo run, dig up every Windows and Word Art cliché ever seen.

http://y2u.be/_IHa-Dnh35c

27

BEASTIE MUPPETS

The Muppets meet the Beastie Boys in an awesome mash-up

Wondering what to search for on YouTube? The answer is
always: try the Muppets. You'll come up with something
special, although perhaps not always as brilliant as this. The
clip is a mash-up, rather than a bona-fide Muppets video,
but it won't fail to raise a smile. This is the Muppets as the
Beastie Boys with the Swedish Chef, Animal and Beaker taking
the microphone in the place of Ad Rock, Mike D, and the late
MCA in their classic rap hit 'So What'cha Want'.

http://y2u.be/kq-VNCGBDRU

HOW TO HANDLE THE JOB INTERVIEW

Actors act out a job interview – as imagined by kids

Kid Snippets is a series of comedy sketches where adults act out children's dialogue in as realistic way possible. This "Job Interview" is a choice episode. It is fascinating to see how toddlers view the world of work and how they imagine an interview situation panning out, but mostly it is very funny and pretty sweet. Does the young fella get the job? You'll have to watch to the end to find out – but there is an intriguing twist. If you like this, there are plenty more episodes: "Band Practice" is another gem.

http://y2u.be/fMX-07Lu6zM

DOGGY STYLE

A high-energy, dog's-eye view of a dash to the beach

The high definition, lightweight GoPro camera has provided a number of YouTube hits from extreme sports feats to stalking sharks. *Run Walter, RUN!* is one of the latest of them to go viral. It features a labrador harnessed with a a GoPro camera to capture a dog's eye view. On a scorching day in Siracusa, Sicily, Walter is let off his leash. He runs from the house with only one aim – to get to the sea as quick as possible. Within 30 seconds, Walter has cleared gates, steps, rocks and bemused sunbathers on the beach to plunge into the Mediterranean for a refreshing swim.

http://y2u.be/UowkIRSDHfs

DOG BLASTS HORN

Impatient hound takes the wheel – and the horn

When Fern the boxer dog got left in the car on her own for too long, she found the ideal way to make her owners pay. Show them up on YouTube! The 18-month-old dog had been left in the car while her owner took in an art gallery in Broughty Ferry, near Dundee in Scotland. Fern was clever enough to know that simply barking at passers-by would not help matters at all, so she climbed in the driver's seat, leaned back and sounded the horn with her paw – repeatedly. Two million views online? That'll teach him not to leave me again!

http://y2u.be/y3xEPpwWGqk

CHANGE THE RECORD

Anyone else sick to death of hearing 'Happy'?

Ready for a quick one? This is the kind of gag that YouTube executes brilliantly. Pharrell William's 'Happy' song is a great track, but not everyone wants to hear it over and over and over again. That's why this perfect 12-second joke hits the nail dead on the head. I won't ruin it, but if you need the background details: the scene is from the classic film *It's A Wonderful Life*; the actress is Donna Reed and the record that is actually playing in the film is 'Buffalo Gals', a popular American folksong.

http://y2u.be/3T-_Ao40CQ4

IRISH WEATHER REPORT

The Irish student's weather comment that went super-viral

When 18-year-old student Ruari McSorley from Derry was interviewed by Ulster Television in Ireland about the recent wave of bad weather, he thought his five minutes of fame might spread around the locality. Instead, the A-level student found his rich Northern Irish accent had become an overnight internet sensation. "Honest to God... it went as far as Japan – overnight! It's mad craic altogether," he is reported to have said. Meanwhile, comments on his suggestion that "You wouldn't be long getting frost bit" ranged from the smitten to the totally bemused.

http://y2u.be/O-m_BPYJG6M

BEST APRIL FOOL

Schoolteacher's phone rule backfires in superb prank

The best pranks are usually the simplest, and this is no exception. A teacher in Aquinas College, in Michigan in the US, had been enforcing his rule that students had to broadcast any calls that they received on speakerphone for the whole class to hear. However, his plan to humiliate them backfires on him spectacularly in this magnificently executed April Fool's prank. There is so much to admire here; from the great set up to the marvellous acting to the generous and good-humoured reaction of the victim.

http://y2u.be/R9rymEWJX38

KISS CAM DRAMA

**When her boyfriend won't play Kiss Cam,
she looks for someone else...**

Is this hilarious clip just too good to be true? Many suspect
this short drama that played out on the big screen at a New
York Knicks basketball match was faked, but so far no one has
admitted as much. An American sports tradition is the kiss
cam – a roving camera picks out a likely couple and when they
appear on the big screen they are supposed to kiss. This guy,
however, wasn't playing – hey, it happens sometimes. Except
his girlfriend wasn't going to be denied some lip action,
so she turns to the man sitting on the other side...

http://y2u.be/Qh0BwuxHRAg

DENTAL DREAMS

A trip to the dentist leaves a woman hilariously distraught

The post-dental anaesthetic clip is a common theme on YouTube. *David After Dentist* and *Unicorn After Wisdom Teeth* have been viewed millions of time and this clip starring Jayci Underwood is hot on their trail. Jayci is a little upset after coming round from the anaesthetic for the simple reason that she hasn't woken up looking like Nicki Minaj and isn't best friends with Ellen DeGeneres. We've all been there – haven't we? And you can also watch a lovely postscript to Jayci's fantasy rant if you search for *A Wisdom Tooth Dream Come True*.

http://y2u.be/idjo2fhLKDY

IT'LL NEVER CATCH ON

Furniture store catalogue ad is a brilliant MacBook parody

The furniture store IKEA prints around 200 million copies of its catalogue every year in 27 different languages. They are clearly not ready to move the whole operation online but have come up with a fabulous way of selling the concept. To launch the 2015 catalogue, IKEA produced this very funny parody of Apple's simplistic and dramatically voiced method of promoting new products. A suitably geeky presenter introduces the new catalogue as a revolutionary gadget. Then he continues to steal Apple's best lines as he explains how the bookbook has "tactile touch technology" and "328 high-definition pages" and how "the battery life is eternal." Spot on!

http://y2u.be/MOXQo7nURs0

LET IT HOWL

Puppy's amazing response to the hit from *Frozen*

We all know that little girls love the film *Frozen* and adore its song 'Let It Go'. But who knew it was a big hit in the pet world too? Here's Oakley, the cutest Australian Shepherd puppy. He's enjoying his nap despite Charli XCX's 'Boom Clap' blaring out of the car speakers. Then, on comes 'Let it Go' and Oakley's little ears perk up. In moments he's up and ready for action, which in his case means howling along to his favourite song. When the track is switched again, Oakley's not interested. He's ready to settle back and dream of his life with Princess Anna.

http://y2u.be/ezz2NqvIORY

BROTHERLY LOVE

He doesn't want another sister and he doesn't care who knows it

It's a magic moment in a parent's life, revealing the gender of your new baby to your children. No wonder this family chose to celebrate the occasion with a cake. Cut the cake open kids and if the filling is pink, it's a girl; if it is blue, it's a boy. Sounds a good plan. The cake is cut and hey, it's pink. At this point they all say how excited they are and tuck in. Er... not exactly. The two sisters seem happy enough, but the brother isn't having it at all. Cue the mightiest anti-girl rant and mother of all sulks.

http://y2u.be/VrAcV2ywnqc

THE FIGHTING IRISH

**Fabulously cross toddler tells off parents
for interrupting her song**

There's nothing a young child hates more than being laughed at
— especially when they are being deadly serious. The two-year-old
girl in this priceless clip is about to sing a song from Disney's
Frozen. Unfortunately, her parents have a fit of the giggles and
are distracting her from her imminent performance. She warns
them, but when they carry on giggling, obviously feels she has
to give them the telling off of a lifetime. Choking themselves,
the naughty step, being sent to their room are all thrown at the
errant grown-ups in the cutest torrent of admonishment
— delivered in the finest Irish brogue.

http://y2u.be/zSyGRut7T0s

SHEENA MAKES IT CLEANER

Flatmate caught cleaning the house in his pants while dancing to '80s hit

It's the morning after a Halloween party and there's a whole lot of cleaning to be done. There's nothing for it, but to get out the mop, put on some happy sounds and get to it – oh, and don't forget to strip down to your briefs too! Jimmy Pope is the almost naked guy in question, dancing and mopping away to Sheena Easton's 1980 hit 'Morning Train (Nine to Five)' – until he realizes his flatmate has been filming him all the time. When this clip went viral in November 2014, Sheena pronounced Jimmy's performance as "adorable" and 'Morning Train' briefly troubled the charts again.

http://y2u.be/cAs7qiQgi38

ANCHORS AWAY!

News presenters' under-the-table live reaction to earthquake

Those brave news reporters are always willing to put themselves in severe danger to bring us the latest news. The presenters on the news desk, however, don't appear to have the same dedication. An earthquake rumbled through Los Angeles in March 2014 just as news anchors Chris Schauble and Megan Henderson were delivering the headlines on TV station KTLA. At the first signs of the light earthquake, the pair shot below their glass table, only reappearing when the momentary shaking halted. Best of all is Chris's unwitting impersonation of YouTube's famous *Dramatic Chipmunk* as his eyes bug out on first sensing the quake.

http://y2u.be/KiB7ny52-xw

CLIPS DON'T LIE

University a cappella group's sensational mash-up of Shakira hits

---

Out of the Blue, an a cappella group made up of students at Oxford University, have tasted success before. They appeared on *Britain's Got Talent* in 2011 and reached the semi-finals with a cappella versions of songs such as Lady Gaga's 'Poker Face' and Justin Timberlake's 'SexyBack'. However, even they were amazed at the reaction to the video of their mash-up of Shakira's hits. Doing their best impression of Shakira's own moves, they shook their stuff across the lawns and along the streets of Oxford, moving Shakira herself to tweet to her 26.2 million followers: "Hey @ooboxford, we LOVE your a capella Shak medley."

http://y2u.be/bRWVMPnByzo

CRY BABY

Devil baby scares the life out of New York City in an awesome prank

---

When this clip appeared in 2014, it was instantly acclaimed as one of the greatest ever pranks. A remote controlled pram, complete with a realistic baby, cruises the streets of New York. When anyone foolish takes a closer look, the terrifying baby sits up and lets out an ear-piercing scream. Like some possessed infant, it is also capable of spewing out an unidentifiable liquid, giving the finger to a police car and uttering obscenities. The prank was part of a publicity campaign for *Devil's Due*, a now mostly forgotten horror film, but the clip continues to clock up hits.

http://y2u.be/yNz_9eSUMKg

HUMANS RULE!

Extreme sports highlights from the always excellent People Are Awesome

---

The People are Awesome productions are one of the most eagerly awaited videos on the whole of YouTube. Posted at the end of each year, the videos are a celebration of the physical capability of the human body and the unquenchable ambition of the human spirit. This takes the form of clips of people running, jumping, somersaulting, riding, throwing and generally performing a host of almost unbelievable feats. All expertly edited to an upbeat musical track — this year it's 'Heroes (We Could Be)' by Alesso Featuring Tove Lo. Both mesmeric and inspiring to watch, it had racked up three million views within a month of being posted.

http://y2u.be/VWf8CXwPoql

SKY-HIGH SELFIE

Taking a crazy selfie from the very top of a skyscraper

Vertigo sufferers, beware! This clip makes even the most level-headed of us take a firm grip on the arms of the chair. Don't get taken in by the casual banana-eating that appears to be taking place between a few friends. These kids have climbed to the very top of The Center, one of the tallest skyscrapers in Hong Kong to have their picnic. Standing precariously 346 metres (1,135 feet) above the Hong Kong streets, Daniel Lau lifts his selfie stick. It's a wonderful view of the city, but you just want him to get down quickly and safely!

http://y2u.be/82SDk1kInvl

DIRT LUMPS?

Lip reading goes very wrong again with more priceless made-up quotes

---

Possibly this is even funnier if you are familiar with these American Football stars, but it's still pretty hilarious. The Bad Lip Reading people do what they say – they provide lip reading interpretations of the sportsmen and coaches and get it very, very wrong. How else could they come out with such gems as "I once got a rake and I killed a snowman"? Or "You made a recipe and then you invented dirt lumps"? If you like this, there are plenty of other Bad Lip Reading videos, including fun takes on *The Hunger Games* and *Game of Thrones*.

http://y2u.be/OTRmyXX6ipU

PANDA PLAY

Panda cub Bao Bao experiences snow for the very first time

Sixteen-month-old Bao Bao is a female Giant Panda cub who lives at the National Zoo in Washington DC. There are only around 2,000 giant pandas left alive in the world and a few hundred of them, like Bao Bao, survive in captivity. In her natural mountain habitat in China she would experience cold and snowy winters, but it wasn't until January 2015 that she first witnessed the white stuff at the zoo. The excited Bao Bao ventured out to experience it for the very first time, tumbling down the hill in her outdoor enclosure, climbing trees and pouncing on her mother Mei Xiang.

http://y2u.be/HQZ3-ODOml0

SISTER ACT

A singing nun's breathtaking debut on *The Voice* in Italy

Sister Cristina Scuccia is a devout nun following the Ursuline order
in Rome. She is also the reigning champion of the Italian version of
The Voice and now a star in her home country. This clip is the first
time most of the country saw Sister Scuccia. She wowed the judges
with her performance of 'No One' by Alicia Keys in this blind audition
and shocked them again when they turned round to discover she
was a nun. Cristina progressed through the competition singing
'Livin' on a Prayer', 'Flashdance – What a Feeling' and even duetting
with Kylie – all available to view on YouTube.

http://y2u.be/TpaQYSd75Ak

FOLLOWING COMPLEX INSTRUCTIONS...

**An instructional video on making toast –
for the hard of thinking**

There is a wealth of really useful tutorials available on YouTube
from how to change a carburettor to how to perform brain
surgery. But seriously? *How to Make Toast From Bread*? It is
not even a joke – the woman giving the complex instructions
("take your slices of bread and put them in the toaster slots") is
completely serious (if somewhat lacking in on-screen charisma).
The Huffington Post went to far as to call it "the most pointless
video on YouTube". I haven't managed to find them, but
there are probably instructional videos on "how to breathe"
or "making a glass of water from water".

http://y2u.be/rJQpyIIV3-s

FUNKY PRESIDENT

Obama sings 'Uptown Funk' in just about the coolest mash-up ever

You might love the original of this tune, but this version from a newcomer to the pop scene is so catchy you might actually prefer it! Barrackdubs have created a successful YouTube channel by editing together the smallest of snippets from President Barack Obama's speeches to make popular songs. Obama's "versions" of hits from Taylor Swift, Lady Gaga and Justin Timberlake were pretty popular and his 'Get Lucky' garnered over 11 million views, but this take on 'Uptown Funk' looks like being the biggest ever. Just to watch the President of the USA saying, "I'm too hot, hot damn!" is worth a minute of anyone's time.

http://y2u.be/wSnx4V_RewE

MAGICIANS VS VAMPIRES

**The Hogwarts crew take on the Twilight
gang in a fantasy dance-off**

This video is like some fantastic dream you had but couldn't
quite remember. How else would Harry, Hermione and Ron from
Harry Potter face off against *Twilight*'s Bella, Edward and Jacob
in the middle of a mystical wood? As the rivals meet head-on,
it's time for a dance-off – with an umbrella-wielding Hagrid on
the decks. Songwriting duo Scott & Brendo penned the catchy
number to accompany this wilderness dance battle. Who wins
this ultimate clash of magicians and vampires? You'll have to
stick it out until the unlikely twist to find out!

http://y2u.be/_bcncbwlXR4

SQUEAK UP, MORGAN!

Honey-voiced Morgan Freeman in high-pitched helium experiment

Oscar-winning actor Morgan Freeman has one of the most distinctive voices on the planet. So calm, comforting and honey-coated are his vocal tones that he often provides voice-overs as God or an all-seeing narrator. So, it's even funnier to see Morgan Freeman indulging in the old party trick of breathing in helium from a balloon in order to make his voice go squeaky. A word of warning: once the illusion is shattered, you might never see him in the same light again; it could ruin your enjoyment of schmaltzy nature films and credit card adverts forever.

http://y2u.be/DCpsusTta4w

CAN YOU HACK IT?

Testing out some life hacks and bizarre hints as posted on the internet

A "life hack" is a trick, skill or technique that makes some aspect of people's life that little bit easier. The internet is full of them, but who knows which are truly useful and which are just myths. That's just what the incredibly popular YouTube channel mental_floss test in this entertaining, and occasionally useful, weekly series. For instance, can you amplify laptop speakers with two halves of a cardboard coffee cup? Can you open a beer with a phone recharger? Or can you use tortilla chips as fire kindling? Those and other life hacks are all put to the test in 10 minutes of fun.

http://y2u.be/3fQIYYZQBM4

CAN YOU HANDLE THE TRUTH?

A film trailer for *Lord of the Rings* that tells it like it is

The Screen Junkies channel run the Honest Trailers series presenting trailers that tell the truth about famous films. With the classic baritone voiceover used in so many blockbuster films, they deliver an amusing and wry, if totally cynical, overview – trashing the acting, direction, special effects, merchandising and especially the sequels of your favourite films. This one takes aim at the *Lord of the Rings* series of films but there are no sacred cows – *Skyfall*, *Game of Thrones*, *The Lego Movie*, even classics like *Ghostbusters* and *Star Wars* – all are dismissed with the same caustic humour.

http://y2u.be/AOli9SjJvgU

COP SHAKES IT OFF

Alone in his police car, a cop gets his funk on to Taylor Swift

Lip-syncing is one of YouTubers' favourite pastimes, but you'll search long and hard to find a better one than this. The Dover Police Department in Delaware announced that they had been reviewing dashcam footage from their police vehicles and claimed to have found "something quite amusing". The footage featured a police officer named Jeff Davis, who has been with the department for 19 years. Alone in the car he was singing along to Taylor Swift's 'Shake It Off' in an extravagant, sometimes camp, magnificent style. Even Taylor herself was forced to retweet the video, saying: "LOLOLOLOL THE SASS." Whatever that means!

http://y2u.be/8XFBUM8dMqw

SMEAGOL HATES HALLOWEEN

When a hairless cat freaks out at owner's Halloween costume

This is wrong in so many ways. Firstly, you really shouldn't tease your pets, they are as worthy of respect as your fellow humans. Secondly, is it really fair naming your hairless sphynx cat Smeagol after the creepy creature in *Lord of the Rings*? And, finally, exactly when is it right for an (almost) naked man to put on a huge werewolf head? OK, that's the worthy stuff dealt with. Now sit back and watch an hugely entertaining short clip of an owner spooking the living daylights out of his cat. There's a Part Two as well if you like this kind of thing!

http://y2u.be/hZQd4u-AOKU

MR GARVEY CALLS THE REGISTER

The original hilarious sketch featuring the now famous Substitute Teacher

Keegan-Michael Key and Jordan Peele are the stars of the hit American comedy sketch show that is broadcast on Comedy Central. Their sketches on YouTube are big hits and none bigger than this short sketch about a substitute teacher. Mr Garvey is a veteran of teaching in inner-city schools and is clearly having trouble with the culture of his new, mostly white, middle-class students. To begin with, he can't even manage to pronounce the names of some his students correctly. There are more Substitute Teacher sketches on YouTube and rumours that Mr Garvey is about to star in his own film.

http://y2u.be/Dd7FixvoKBw

TAKING THE PISTE

A day in the life journal of outrageous GoPro skiing stunts

Don't be fooled into thinking this is just another of those head-cam filmed show-off skiers videos. Well, it is — but Candide Thovex puts together the most entertaining GoPro experiences ever. His video takes us on a journey around the slopes of Val Blanc in France as he performs one outrageous trick after another; flipping, spinning and jumping clear over people on the piste below. He weaves through incredibly tight gaps between trees and doesn't even stop when the snow runs out, continuing to ski on grass and a rocky tunnel. Stay on for the amazing finale as Candide ends the video in hilarious style.

http://y2u.be/yKP7jQknGjs

PARALLEL WORLD

The World Record Tightest Parallel Park

Try this manoeuvre when you're faced with a tight parking space at the local supermarket car park. In front of a live audience at the 2015 Performance Car Show, British stunt driver Alastair Moffatt slid a Fiat 500 1.2 Cult into the narrowest of parallel parking spaces. Moffat's magnificent handbrake turn was made in a completely standard car with the exception of an enhanced steering wheel and pumped-up tyre pressures. Taking a space just 7.5 centimetres (2.95 inches) longer than the car enabled Moffat to reclaim a world record that had been taken by a Chinese stunt driver. He bested the record by half a centimetre.

http://y2u.be/VSp1olKp_f0

SPARKLING REVENGE

Boy executes wicked glitter bomb revenge on his nosey dad

This clip was so popular that the company selling the "glitter bombs" were overwhelmed with pranksters wanting to spring a sparkling surprise on their friends. The lad posting the clip said he was so sick of his father opening his mail that he decided to give him a surprise. The company in question supply tubes full of glitter with a spring-loaded device. So, he ordered himself a tube and set his camera up ready for when his dad got nosey.

It couldn't have worked better – the "glitter bomb" showers hundreds of shimmering pieces down on the man and his desk.

http://y2u.be/yOyjATpkDxM

CUPCAKE KID

Three-year-old argues like a pro

He's three years old — and as cute as a button — and he's got every trick in the book. It's not exactly the UN, but Mateo is in trouble for trying to sneak a cupcake and seems sure he can argue his way out of it. "Linda, honey, honey, look, look at this," he pleads with his mum as he puts forward a case that since he'd already eaten lunch, a cake would surely suffice. And he's ready to use his oratory skills to protect his brother from punishment too: "But he's my little Pa-Paps!" he says. A legal career beckons...

http://y2u.be/TP8RB7UZHKI

THE APPARENTLY KID

The over-earnest boy who won the internet's heart

The kid's a natural, they often say. But Noah Ritter really is. In a short local news interview at a county fair in Pennsylvania, five-year-old Noah makes it look like he's been as it all his short life even though he (three times) reassures his interviewer that it's the first time he has been on live television. But what sealed his internet fame was his use of the word "apparently". Eight times it pops up in the one-minute interview — but on the US *Today Show* he admitted he was tired of saying the word "apparently", even confessing, "I don't know what it means."

http://y2u.be/rz5TGN7eUcM

OSTRICH DROPS THE BEAT!

The big bird gets into the groove

The ostrich has a reputation for putting its head in the sand, but now we know the truth: it just wasn't hearing the right tunes. This bird is more than willing to shake a tail feather when the beat kicks in. A typical piece of YouTube opportunism matched up this footage with a great soundtrack and a meme was born. Of course, what is really happening is that the male ostrich is performing a common courtship ritual – he will alternate his wing beats until he attracts a mate. But why ruin a good clip with wildlife facts!

http://y2u.be/6BNVKEaYOVs

HIP, HOP... SPLASH

A cool rapper takes an unscheduled swim...

His record company describe him as a "street cat", but rap star Presto Flo clearly lacks the balance of the feline. The hip-hop artist took an uncool dive when on a photo shoot in Clearwater, Florida. Presto was doing his gangsta poses on the seafront, when a strong gust of wind blew his cap seawards. Reaching out to grab his headwear, he stumbled backwards, and the next thing he knew he was heading for the drink. Poor old Presto landed on an oyster bed and cut his hands and legs, but that's what you get for living life on the edge.

http://y2u.be/c7eXj92qqbE

HOLE IN ONE

Builder drops in at the golf shop

Security cameras captured this gem in a golf shop. The still
of the shop is broken by a tremendous kerfuffle – which we
soon realize is the figure of Ryan falling through the ceiling.
Ironically, Ryan had been upstairs fixing the wires to the
camera. Now, Ryan is not alone. Working with him is his mate,
Billy, who seems pretty unsurprised to see his friend lying in
the rubble. "Hey Ryan," says Billy... As the casual conversation
continues with the addition of a ridiculous comment from a
customer in the shop, a YouTube classic is born.

http://y2u.be/EXvT8QbEMfQ

GRANDMOTHER'S DAY

A goal-scoring footballer wins the hearts of grannies everywhere

Modern footballers get a bad press with all their posturing, diving and fake injuries. So let's salute Roma's Alessandro Florenzi. After scoring a goal against Cagliari, Florenzi didn't tear off his shirt or perform some over-rehearsed celebration. Instead he headed for the stands. Those waiting to see which blonde beauty he was headed for were gobsmacked to find him pick out and hug an elderly lady in the crowd. It was Florenzi's 82-year-old grandmother, who was watching him play for the first ever time. Back on the pitch, Florenzi got a yellow card. These referees have no heart.

http://y2u.be/C-ERsWiD9CQ

YOU'RE FAT, YOU'RE FAT, FAT, FAT

Witty and catchy mash-up of over-heated daytime TV debate

Our children are becoming more obese by the year. Whose fault is it? Is it our responsibility? What can we do about it? On a debate on the ITV show *This Morning*, the ever charming Katie Hopkins and journalist Sonia Paulton nearly came to blows over the issue. As insults got more and more personal (it's available to view on YouTube), presenters Phillip Schofield and Holly Willoughby did their best to mediate, but it was left to master mash-up merchant Dave Wollacott to put the whole thing into perspective with his silly, hilarious and even catchy version.

http://y2u.be/Hjiw6gmO4qQ

PRETTY ANGRY POLLY

Parrot takes exception to theme from *Titanic*

Gentle music is meant to have a calming effect on animals, but we all have our limits. Kiki the parrot usually enjoys the music her owner plays along to on his violin. However, on this occasion, from the very opening notes of Celine Dion's 'My Heart Will Go On' – the theme song from the film *Titanic* – it is clear something is ruffling Kiki's feathers. By the time our virtuoso violinist has joined in, she is positively apoplectic and forced to take action. Listen out too for her mocking words at the end of the incident – priceless!

http://y2u.be/R1XiT25JIXA

GIRL POW-AHHHHH!

French feminist makes a stand – and a fall

The fight for equal rights for women takes many forms and so we should salute the efforts of the mademoiselle in this video. She feels it is time to make a stand against er... well, against the fact that it was just men (and not women) being nominated to be filmed jumping into rivers to be posted on Facebook. All power to her, why should gender make any difference to making an ass of yourself? So, very cleverly, she does not just jump into the water, she magnificently makes more of an ass of herself than any of her male counterparts...

http://y2u.be/kt5UaPFiYLE

HEAD IN THE CLOUDS

Stunning footage of Grand Canyon Total Cloud Inversion

Visitors who had travelled to the Grand Canyon in December 2014 didn't get the wonderful view of the immense canyon they might have imagined. Instead, they were treated to a pretty awesome and rare weather phenomenon called a "total cloud inversion". The canyon looked like a huge witch's cauldron as swirling clouds gradually filled it to the brim. The total cloud inversion usually happens every few years and occurs when warm air is sandwiched by cool air from the top and from below. The spectacular sight occurs as clouds are trapped in the canyon by the relatively heavier, drier air.

http://y2u.be/zF8LUy1LJjs

HAVING A WHALE OF A TIME

There's a killer whale under the inflatable!

Eric Martin, his son Cody, and their friend were enjoying a trip in their inflatable boat in the waters around Southern California's Redondo Beach when they were approached by a pod of killer whales. The boat, measuring just 3 metres (10 feet), was dwarfed by the Orca whales, who came right up close to investigate. They come face to face with the trippers and even swim right under the inflatable. The whales were later identified as a "friendly" family group who had a reputation for approaching boats – but never one as small as this.

http://y2u.be/Uv7pqqbXwQl

THE LIVING AND JUMPING DEAD

Zombie chase game comes to life in parkour thriller

This video combines three YouTube favourites — games trailers, zombies and parkour — and comes up with a winner. This live-action short film is based on the game *Dying Light*, a survival video game, and does a fabulous job of bringing the excitement of the game to life. Shot on the rooftops of Cambridge, the trailer, like the game, is shot in a first-person perspective with a non-stop, parkour-style zombie chase. Well directed and exciting, the video was well received; it went viral instantly, with over a million views in its first 24 hours of being online.

http://y2u.be/4NUOjzbFj1g

¡GIGGLES

Giggling "Apple Engineer" recounts the invention of the MacBook

Are you ready to watch this video on your new MacBook? If so, you might want to know how the revolutionary computer came into being. This Spanish "Apple engineer" spills the beans on the 2015 MacBook. And it's hilarious. The video is actually a subtitled clip of an old TV interview with Spanish comedian Juan Joya Borja, known as El Risitas, or The Giggles, for obvious reasons. The enthusiasm with which the YouTube have greeted the video has led many to believe it is the new *Downfall* – the subtitled Hitler meme that wouldn't go away.

http://y2u.be/KHZ8ek-6ccc

A WOMAN'S TOUCH

Fantastic FIFA-acclaimed goal by Irish footballer Stephanie Roche

Cristiano Ronaldo and Lionel Messi are not the first footballers to have their heads turned by an attractive blonde in a designer dress. But the woman who caught their eye at the Ballon d'Or awards ceremony in Zurich was award nominee Stephanie Roche. The fantastic goal she scored for Peamount against Wexford Youths in October 2013 had been nominated for the award for the best goal of the season, and she had become the first female to be named a finalist. Roche missed out on the award but was named runner-up. Shortly after, she signed a contract with professional US team Houston Dash.

http://y2u.be/qpBvBRn4juw

BLIND FAITH

I Trust You, Do You Trust Me? Hug Me – Social Experiment

"I am a Muslim. I am labelled as a terrorist. I trust you. Do you trust me? Give me a hug." Canadian Muslim Mustafa Mawla was taking part in the Blind Trust Project – a social experiment "to break down barriers and eliminate the fear and ignorance projected towards Muslims and Islam." He was filmed as he stood blindfolded with outstretched arms on a busy Toronto street. In these days of mistrust and suspicion how would he fare? Would Mustafa be shunned or embraced by the people of Toronto? Two million people have already watched the surprising results of this intriguing video.

http://y2u.be/epdkdbMEh0c

WHAM BAM

Teenage rap duo Bars & Melody
wow Cowell with anti-bullying song

Although Bars and Melody (BAM for short) only came third in the 2014 series of *Britain's Got Talent*, there is every sign that they could end up as the de facto winners. This YouTube video of their audition performance, in which Simon Cowell pressed the legendary Golden Buzzer, has already racked up over 65 million views and they subsequently signed a record deal with Cowell's label. Consisting of rapper Leondre Devries and singer Charlie Lenehan, BAM performed a song based on Twista and Faith Evans' 'Hope', with Devries replacing the original verses with ones protesting against bullying.

http://y2u.be/g3Rf5qDuq7M

GHOST CITY

**Footage from the empty streets of a
twenty-first-century city in China**

There is something decidedly spooky about the city of Ordos in
Northern China. There are no creaking old buildings or rattling
gates, for this is a sparkling modern city, but nevertheless it
is the biggest ghost town in the world. Built for over a million
people to live and work in it, Ordos was to be the jewel of a
booming Inner Mongolia. Unfortunately, this futuristic metropolis
that rises out of the deserts of northern China, never took off.
Only 2% of its buildings were ever inhabited; the rest has largely
been empty or has been abandoned mid-construction.

http://y2u.be/0brcZTVde-I

JENGA FAIL

**Reporter checks out world record Jenga tower
– with interesting consequences...**

If this is for real it's the best fail on YouTube – if it's fake, it's a
brilliant prank. So either way it's worth a couple of minutes of your
time. It concerns a model of the Leaning Tower of Pisa made out
of around 12,000 Jenga bricks. It looks great, if worryingly built in
the middle of a busy university library. The would-be record breaker
just has to wait a week for the appearance of the Guinness record-
approving officials to seal his place in history. Plenty of time, then,
to entertain reporters from the local television network...

http://y2u.be/3Y6Lbgs2g4A

MEAN STREETS

The much-discussed *10 Hours of Walking in NYC as a Woman* video

One of the YouTube stories of 2014, this shocking video simply showed a woman walking alone through the streets of New York City. Over ten hours a secret camera filmed 24-year-old actress Shoshana B Roberts walking through various neighbourhoods of the city. She remains straight-faced and silent as male strangers greet her, make comments on her personal appearance, and even walk alongside her for several minutes. It creates a powerful message on street harassment and has provoked debate and parodies as well as many copycat versions of walking in NYC as a gay man, a Jew, in a habib and others.

http://y2u.be/b1XGPvbWnOA

COW IN THE HOUSE

**"Ooops, I let the cow in..." And so begins
a beguiling six minutes**

What begins as parental investigation turns into one of the
cutest videos ever in this everyday tale of family life. Billie Jo
Decker has discovered the family's calf in the house and there
is only one way it could it have got there: her five-year-old
daughter, Breanna, let it in. As the cute-as-a-button child tries
to talk her way out of trouble, her mother keeps the camera
rolling. What emerges is a special bond between Brenna and
the young cow as she snuggles up to the surprise house guest.
As her mother says, "That's is just too sweet."

http://y2u.be/M5H7uMq3mS8

WHEN I GROW UP...

**Star comedian Tim Minchan's life lessons
for students at his old university**

"I didn't make the bit of me that works hard, any more than I
made the bit of me that ate too much burgers instead of going
to lectures." As a former student at the University of Western
Australia, Tim Minchin, composer, lyricist, comedian, actor and
writer of the smash hit musical *Matilda*, was invited to give
address at the university's graduation ceremony. His inspirational
ten-minute speech in which he offers up nine life lessons to the
students is full of the wit, intelligence and modesty we have
come to expect from this consummate performer.

http://y2u.be/yoEezZD71sc

HIT THE DECK

Marvel at the spellbinding talents of cardistry artists in Singapore

Skilful, dexterous and fascinating to watch, cardistry is a fast-growing art. While card magic uses the handling of playing cards as an illusionary art, cardists or "flourishers" manipulate cards in order to put on a show of skill. Flourishing techniques include shuffles, one-handed cuts, armspreads, springs, shapes displays and any number of nimble-fingered twists and turns of the pack. This video features a sextet of cardistry artists in Singapore as they show off their fascinating and hypnotic ability to manipulate cards, but if you fancy learning some smooth moves yourself, check out the thevirts channel which is full of fabulous tutorials.

http://y2u.be/w_M_aRtX-bA

SWEET DREAMS, KIDS

Liam Neeson Reads a Bedtime Story

If you are looking for a bedtime story to help the kids settle down to sleep, then skip this one. However, if you want a good chuckle, it could be the perfect clip for you – especially if you are a fan of movie hero Liam Neeson. While on US chat show *Jimmy Kimmel Live!*, Liam took time out to read the children's story *Five Little Monkeys*. The stern voiced Irishman would surely be perfect for the story of bed-jumping monkeys being told off by the doctor. It does seem that way, until the actor loses patience with the repetitive story...

http://y2u.be/IQZAUVOMoGk

RAPPY EVER AFTER

Two of Disney's prime princesses battle it out in a rhyming rap face-off

"Of course you're bitter, I'm the Number One star. Pumpkin carriage, perfect marriage; no one cares who you are." Cinderella gets straight to the point as she goes head to head in a rap battle with Belle. The Beast's beauty gives as good as she gets: "Your tale's as old as time, sets us back fifty years. Do your chores, clean the floors, 'til a man just appears?" Rap battles are all over YouTube, but this is a pretty neat example. It is witty, bitchy and smoothly performed by Buffy actress Sarah Michelle Gellar (Cinderella) and Whitney Avalon (Belle).

http://y2u.be/VeZXQf77hhk

SIGNED AND SEALED

The world is reimagined for the hard-of-hearing in a poignant prank

Some ads are just too good to ignore. To promote their video call centre for people with hearing problems, Samsung Turkey came up with a heart-warming stunt. Muharrem is an ordinary guy living in Istanbul who happens to have impaired hearing. As we watch him go about his daily routine, we see Muharrem surprised, and slightly bemused, to find strangers around him using sign language to communicate with him and make his day easier. When the set-up is revealed, Muharrem's reactions are priceless. If this doesn't bring a lump to your throat, you surely have no heart.

http://y2u.be/UrvaSqN76h4

KNUCKLE DOWN

What happens to your knuckles when you crack them?

Up in the Top 10 ways of irritating your parents is cracking your knuckles. They will tell you that you will dislocate your fingers or that you will end up with arthritis. This video tells you what is happening to your hands when you make the popping sound that drives everyone around you to distraction. And it compares the hands of a man who has cracked the knuckles on just one hand, all his life. Is it just a harmless habit or will you spend your later years in agony? I think you need to know...

http://y2u.be/n3lYmdy6d4Y

SQUEAK UP FOR BRITNEY

**Britney's classic – without the music,
but with the jumpsuit squeaks!**

They just won't leave Britney alone! YouTuber Mario Wienerroither
has made an art form out of musicless music videos, but his
execution of Britney Spears' 'Oops!...I Did It Again' is surely his
finest 60 seconds yet. Wienerroither strips the beats and lyrics from
an uncut shot of Spears dancing around her Mars ship and inserts
some rather too realistic squeaks and creaks that emerge from
her famous bright red vinyl jumpsuit. If you enjoy this, have a look
at Wienerroither's other videos, including David Bowie and Mick
Jagger's 'Dancing in the Street', and the Village People's 'YMCA'.

http://y2u.be/cm0evQaHIE4

THE SOUND OF SILENCE

A priceless parody of all those *For the First Time...* videos

---

YouTube videos have borne witness to quite a few miracle moments. Cameras have recorded the first seconds when, thanks to modern science, previously blind people have recovered their sight or those with hearing impediments have heard their first sounds. This is something equally or even more special. It features a father of four who has not heard silence for ten years. The cameras are there as, thanks to the latest technology, he is finally able to hear it again. Oh, and it contains a bad swear word, so best avoid this clip, if that upsets you.

http://y2u.be/18kqcczy6MQ

MILKY COLA SLUDGE

Interesting experiment showing the result of mixing milk and cola

---

If you enjoyed the cola and mentos experiment, this might be up your street. This video shows what happens when you mix cola and milk and let it stand for five or six hours. As you will see, some pretty strange science stuff goes on, leaving you with an almost clear liquid and a few centimetres of browny sludge at the base of the bottle. Basically, the phosphoric acid contained in the cola strips away the protein molecules from the milk, this dense sludge sinks to the bottom, and the remaining liquid becomes lighter and floats on top.

http://y2u.be/NhofonPRrFM

HOUDINI-PUS

**Amazing footage of an octopus's escape
through the smallest of holes**

The things you can learn on YouTube! Would you believe a huge
octopus can squeeze itself through a small letterbox size gap?
Well, the proof is here in Chance Miller's amazing footage of
an octopus escape through an unbelievably small hole on a
boat sailing near the Chiswell Islands, Alaska. The octopus is
nature's great escape artist. Its long tentacles can feel the way
out and its complete lack of an internal skeleton means that
once it has the only hard part — its beak — through, it can just
pour the rest of its body through any gap.

http://y2u.be/9yHlsQhVxGM

THE OSCARS GO GAGA

Lady Gaga does *The Sound of Music* at the Oscars – what a star!

The Hollywood Hills were alive with the sound of music as Lady Gaga wowed the millions watching the 2015 Oscars. Eschewing her usual flamboyant outfits, Lady Gaga took the stage wearing a Swan Lake-esque gown (perhaps a nod to "girls in white dresses"?). The singer sang a medley of hits from the Academy Award-winning film *The Sound Of Music* to celebrate the its fiftieth anniversary. Her performance included 'The Sound Of Music', 'Climb Every Mountain', and 'My Favourite Things'/ And, to cap it all, she was joined by the film's original star, Julie Andrews.

http://y2u.be/dSgQqSmZz6k

MEALS ON WHEELS

Panic in the car as a safari park lion opens the door!

"Keep your doors and windows closed at all times" read the signs at safari parks. We've seen the way those pesky monkeys swarm over any vehicle, just looking for a way in. However, it seems it's not the monkeys we needed to be worried about, it's the lions. This video, shot on a safari park in South Africa, shows a family excitedly taking snaps of a pride of lions. A curious lioness ambles over to cast an eye over the visitors, then suddenly, like a concrete jungle carjacker, she opens the back passenger door. Cue panic amongst the humans...

http://y2u.be/yeaztQK9If0

INSTANT FRIED SHRIMPS

**You won't believe how they make these
fried prawns in just seconds**

If you see one of these for sale in the electrical goods aisle at
your local supermarket, I suggest you snap it up. Then you too
could be making battered fried shrimp in three seconds flat. You
don't need to speak Japanese to be amazed by this video (it is a
commercial for a mobile phone company, if you are interested).
Just watch as the shrimp are blasted through an air tunnel of
flour, egg and bread crumbs before hitting the flames and the
plate. That looks like pretty tasty Ishrimp tempura to me.

http://y2u.be/IkaIoH6Um60

PRETTY IN INK

In slow motion, the dispersal of coloured ink is a wonder to behold

---

The Slo Mo Guys – Gavin Free and Dan Gruchy – take a £100,000 high speed camera to film hundreds of times slower than you can see with your own eyes. The most popular of their videos find them exploding a water melon with elastic bands, heading a football and trying to burst a giant water balloon. In this excellent edition, they squirt coloured ink into a tank of water and film the result at 1,000 frames per second. The slow motion replay of the ink spreading in the water is, as the title suggests, completely hypnotic.

http://y2u.be/gzkB574jivA

THICK AS A BRICK

Ireland's stupidest criminal attempts to break into a car...

The guy in this video achieved the kind of fame you don't want when he was labelled Ireland's stupidest criminal in 2015. He tried to break into a car by throwing a brick through the window. Unfortunately things took a turn for the worse for the would-be thief. He was found lying in a pool of his own blood by the car's owner after it rebounded off the window and smashed into his own face. Gerry Brady, owner of the car told the *Irish Independent*: "You should have heard the gardaí [Irish Police] laughing when they saw the video. They were in stitches."

http://y2u.be/dxSTDTVNpK4

EMMA TELLS THE WORLD

Harry Potter girl's passionate UN speech on gender equality

"Who is this Harry Potter girl? What is she doing at the U.N.?"
Actress Emma Watson, who played Hermione in the *Harry Potter*
films, pre-empted the question that she assumed many would
ask. The answer was that she was a United Nations Goodwill
Ambassador for Women and she was there to speak up for the
He For She campaign, which calls for men to support gender
equality. Watson, who confessed she was extremely nervous,
surprised many with a moving and emotional speech that is
worth watching right through to the powerful parting message.

http://y2u.be/Q0Dg226G2Z8

COPY CAT

Anything a dog can do, a cat can do too...

Is it a cat that thinks it is a dog? A cat that thinks it can do whatever a dog does? Or a dog stuck in a cat's body? Whatever it is, it's a fun video watch. Lucy and Phoenix the Rottweilers line up on the floor ready to perform a trick. Next to them lies a cat named Didga. On the command each of the dogs performs a perfect "Roll Over". Then it's Didga's turn. How good a copycat is she? We're about to find out.

http://y2u.be/a_MqiGb0Qzk

BUFFALO KISSES

**Snog, feed or avoid? A country park encounter
with an amorous buffalo**

Buffalos – the oversize bulls common to the USA – aren't
famous for their romantic spirit. They are, however, partial to
a piece of bread. Caroline Walker Evans posted this video on
YouTube and called it *Buffalo Kisses*. As she and a friend drove
through a country park, a couple of buffalo shuffled alongside
her car. She decided to feed one a piece of bread. The next
thing she knows, Caroline has a big hairy face poking through
the window and a huge tongue heading for her cheek. Was it
looking for more bread – or could it be love?

http://y2u.be/HK4cjWvkmI8

SPEED DATING

The blind date where the guys end up shutting their eyes in fear!

The guys in this clip, all aspiring actors, believe they're auditioning for a new dating show. They're a macho bunch and they have no qualms about taking a ride with their attractive blonde date behind the wheel of a brand new Ford Mustang. One describes himself as a "ninja"; another says, "I'm a very adventurous guy"; and one of her dates even offers to drive and show her "what this thing can do". What they don't know is that their date is professional stunt driver Prestin Persson – and she is about to give them the ride of their life...

http://y2u.be/3Nyr1Ao7iZA

THE DRESS THAT DIVIDED THE WORLD

That dress – and why we saw it in different colours

The whole world was talking about the dress. For once, it wasn't a daring number that a celebrity had worn to an awards ceremony, but a photo of a dress a mother of the bride had sent to her daughter. When the bride and groom looked at the picture, they each saw the image differently. When they posted the image to social media, it divided the world. Some saw a blue and black dress, while others believed they were looking at a white and gold number. How could people see the same picture so differently? This video attempts to answer that question.

http://y2u.be/AskAQwOBvhc

PLAYPIT HOUSE

Honey, I'm home – but she doesn't know home is filled with plastic play balls!

Roman Atwood is a serial prankster. His YouTube channel is full of hilarious stunts and this is one of the favourites. While his wife was out at work, Roman ordered a truck full of plastic play balls and turned his house into a giant play pit. He spread over a quarter of a million balls over the floors, then proceeded to dive off the stair balcony into them. When he finds out his wife is on the way home, he prepares a special treat for when she opens the front door. If you enjoy it, check out an extended version on Plastic Ball Prank EXTRAS!!

http://y2u.be/7t0EtKlQxyo

LOVE ALL

12-year-old outplays tennis ace in gripping rally

Roger Federer is arguably the best tennis player in the history of the game. His opponents have searched high and low to find his weak spot – but always in vain. So it was a big surprise to see the great man undone by a stranger from the stands – even more surprising, it was a 12-year-old kid. During an exhibition match at Madison Square Garden, his opponent Grigor Dimitrov let the lad play a point against Federer. The boy doesn't flinch. He lures the Swiss legend to the net with a series of shots and then goes for the kill...

http://y2u.be/hU2jPw0mjaE

GUESS WHO'S COMING FOR DINNER?

A giant grizzly bear fights four wolves for a place at their dinner table

It's only a rotten old carcass, but for a pack of hungry wolves it must have seemed like a banquet. The last thing they wanted was an uninvited guest turning up for supper — least of all a 320-kilogram (50-stone) grizzly bear. This footage of nature at its most raw is compelling but not horrific. The four wolves show no fear in trying to chase the mighty bear away from their food, but equally the grizzly is ready to take them all on. Who wins? Watch to discover a conclusion as fascinating as the fight itself.

http://y2u.be/6rBBPKUpC4E

100 YEARS OF BEAUTY

Time lapse video that illustrates a century of make-up and hair style changes

---

In just one minute of time-lapse footage, a model is transformed by a team of hair and make-up artists into different looks over the span of 100 years. We see make-up and hair routines evolving from 1910 to 2010 as model Nina Carduner appears in everything from the pin-curls and bow lips of the early twentieth century to the moussed-up style of the 1980s, ending with today's natural waves. This video has more than 20 million views and the producers, Cut Video, have followed it up with similar one-minute films.

http://y2u.be/LOyVvpXRX6w

THE DISAPPEARING PETROL CAP

Working out which side the petrol cap is on proves a real problem for one driver

---

Some people don't need a prank to make them look foolish. This unfortunate woman is not the first driver to have driven into a petrol station and parked by a pump, only to find the petrol cap is on the other side of the car. And who wants to risk embarrassment by trying, and failing, to stretch the pump around the other side of the car? Better to get back in and drive round the other way. Only this time, that plan doesn't work. The cap is still on the other side. So she tries again and again and...

http://y2u.be/TfHUsPOCI0A

MUNCHKIN WORKS OUT

It's walkie time for adorable Munchkin, the Teddy Bear shih tzu

---

Now you might find this adorable or you might just think things have gone way too far. Munchkin is a shih tzu dog from South California. She is pretty sweet as it is, but dressed up in her Teddy Bear outfit, and appearing to walk standing up, she pushes the cuteness into the red zone. Munchkin the Teddy Bear made her name as an Instagram sensation but found no problem transferring her skills to YouTube. Here she is working out on the treadmill, and you can also find videos of her on the red carpet, on the beach and out sleighing.

http://y2u.be/mVmBL8B-In0

THE HAMSTER GETS IT

**The sweetest little hamster gets shot –
and pretends to be dead**

Bless YouTube for still being able to come up with videos like this! It's just 16 seconds long but is almost guaranteed to put a smile on your face. In the history of the site we have seen talented cats and dogs and chipmunks pulling dramatic faces but never a hamster with acting skills like this. Some, among the 11 million viewers who have viewed the clip, have contributed their own names for the performing rodent, including Arnold Hamsternegger and Jean Claude Van Hamster. Can you do any better?

http://y2u.be/7nhll1UslDg

HAPPY ANNIVERSARY, YOUTUBE!

A superb montage of ten years of the best ever YouTube clips

On Valentine's Day, 2015 YouTube celebrated its tenth anniversary.
The site has seen an incredible journey from a single upload to the
100 minutes that are posted every minute on the site today. This
three-and-a-half minute clip features many of the best videos to
appear on YouTube: from the original *Me At the Zoo* clip to *Charlie
Bit My Finger*; and from *The Sneezing Baby Panda* to *The Evolution
of Dance*. If you finish this book and are looking for more great
clips, you could do worse than work your way through the playlist
included in the first line of the video information.

http://y2u.be/wPd0MumNLbg

STRANGER THAN STRANGE

Ten photos of mysteries, conspiracies and strange phenomenon that defy explanation

---

If you like a conspiracy theory, you'll love this short video of ten photographs and film clips that have no apparent explanation. They range from a family picture in which a man in a space suit appears to be standing behind a little girl to a mysterious old lady seen calmly taking photographs of the chaos surrounding John F. Kennedy's assassination, as well as pyramids on the moon, sea monsters and the bizarre behaviour of a soon-to-be-murdered woman. Along with the usual puerile comments below the clip, there are some interesting theories that attempt to explain the mysteries.

http://y2u.be/TU5rtGDaE9Y

THE SORRY CAT

**The cat that tries to say sorry –
then thinks better of it...**

There are so many good cat videos on YouTube and plenty of
people watching them. This one has been viewed over seven
million times! It's no wonder, as it has a little of everything;
romance, pathos, violence and, of course, cats. Perhaps we
identify with the kitty who seems desperate to apologize but
continues to get the cold shoulder from his mate. He must have
done something pretty bad to get a serious brush off like that.
Keep watching, though, because the reason this is so popular is
for the excellent and hilarious sting in the tail.

http://y2u.be/yNS7zzIzX-E

PIGS MIGHT SWIM

Swimming with pigs on a paradise beach

Swimming with dolphins is so last decade. Anyone who is anyone these days is swimming with pigs. The beaches and tropical waters of the Bahamas are known as the hang-out of film stars and pop singers, but lesser known are the fellas with whom they have to share the beach. A family of brown and pink pigs and piglets lie in the sun on the sandy white beaches and swim in the surf on Big Major Spot Island. Because they are so friendly and even swim out to greet incoming boats, locals have named the area Pig Beach.

http://y2u.be/BJuL-yK-l8g

STREET FIGHTIN' KANGAS

In a quiet Australian suburb, two kangaroos scrap it out "Thai boxing" style

Street fighting is an ugly thing. It isn't fun, skilful or entertaining to watch – unless it's two kangaroos having a set-to. Here we are in a quiet suburban street with no one around apart from the two marsupials trying to knock the doo-dah out of each other. There's no drunken crowd, mates trying to help with a sneaky kick or girlfriends shouting, "Leave him, Darren, he's not worth it." As far as fights go, it's pretty clean, although there's a couple of blows that look a bit below the pouch.

http://y2u.be/JyqJX7bU0Ws

BOOMERANG BRILLIANCE

Amazing trick shots from a boomerang master

It is not clear just who the guy in these South Korean adverts for Seoul Tourism is, but it is soon obvious that he is a master at his art. If this was in a super-hero blockbuster, you would probably be shaking your head in disbelief at the accuracy with which he wields the boomerang. Using just a plastic version of the weapon, he manages to displace items from the head of someone standing 6 metres (20 feet) away, extinguish a candle and simultaneously burst a two separate balloons using two boomerangs. Is he still as good blindfolded? You better believe it...

http://y2u.be/UzaMDp3dgJc

SKYE'S NO LIMIT

BMX superstar Danny MacAskill returns with a scintillating ride on the Isle of Skye

---

BMX star Danny MacAskill's videos are always slick, beautifully filmed and full of incredible cycling feats. This is no exception, even though Danny swaps his usual urban playground for the breathtaking scenery of the Isle of Skye in his native country, Scotland. In an awesome journey, requiring all of the rider's great technical skills, Danny negotiates the jaged terrain, jumps rocks and rides knife-edge paths next to sheer cliff drops to become the first person to ride the island's Black Cuillin ridge, even climbing with his bike to the infamous "Inaccessible Pinnacle".

http://y2u.be/xQ_IQS3VKjA

JUMP FOR YOUR LIFE

Terrifying footage as a skydivers' plane is caught in a mid-air collision

Watch this in-flight footage of a terrifying mid-air collision 3,660 metres (12,000 feet) above Superior, Wisconsin. Panic sets in when the wings of the small plane burst into flames and the plane careers towards the ground. They had been hit by another plane whose skydivers were joining them in a formation jump. Fortunately, the divers were already on the verge of launching themselves out of the plane and soon the pilot joined them too. Amazingly, there were no fatalities and only minor injuries as the pilot of the other aircraft managed to negotiate his way safely back to the runway.

http://y2u.be/7p6hqMnsLFY

OUT OF THIS WORLD

**TV's Professor Brian Cox's experiment at the
world's biggest vacuum chamber**

TV scientist Professor Brian Cox travelled to the NASA Space
Power Facility near Cleveland, Ohio to test the laws of gravity.
There in the world's biggest vacuum chamber, used to test
spacecraft in space-like conditions, Cox raises a bowling ball
and feathers above the ground and drops them simultaneously.
With no air resistance they seem to fall at the same rate, but as
Professor Cox explains they are not "falling" at all, but "at rest".
As Einstein theorized, you wouldn't know if one of the objects is
moving at all unless there is a "background".

http://y2u.be/E43-CfukEgs

BALLOON TUNE

'80s hit '99 Red Balloons' is played with red balloons

It takes a pretty unique cover song to stand out on YouTube these days. And they don't come much more unique than Toronto-based musician, Andrew Huang's version of Nena's 1980s hit '99 Red Balloons'. Huang's cover of the catchy anti-nuclear ditty is played on… red balloons. His split-screen video shows Andrew and his balloon instruments including bass, snare, melody and drums. Even Nena's vocals are recreated by a careful escape of air from a red balloon. The only criticism he seems to have received is for using just four red balloons. What happened to the other 95?

http://y2u.be/aZND9dApFKU

MINE'S BIGGER THAN YOURS

CCTV footage of an armed robber meeting his match

It's the moment every shop owner dreads – when a customer pulls a gun and demands the contents of the till. Except this shopkeeper in Pennsylvania, USA was prepared for just this situation. Unruffled by the intruder, he calmly reaches down and produces a gun of his own. His weapon certainly looks a whole lot more powerful than the air gun that the would-be thief was touting. The postscript to the video was that the robber was caught nearby after running into a nearby apartment.
The local Police Chief said he was "one of the world's dumbest, and luckiest to be alive, criminals".

http://y2u.be/MLFEpaSAWVk

THE iMAGICIAN

Amazing magician uses his iPad to do more than just play Crossy Road

---

The iGeneration are already pretty taken with their tablets and now they can add magic to the list of iActivities. German magician Simon Plerro performs his tricks with the aid of an iPad and they are pretty stunning. Although he has already been invited to perform at Apple stores and is the Angry Birds official magician (who knew they had one?), this video features Simon's big break as he demonstrates his iMagic on *The Ellen DeGeneres Show* in the US. Using Apple's tablet along with traditional sleight-of-hand techniques, he pours drinks into and out of the tablet and wows his host with a pretty amazing selfie stunt.

http://y2u.be/b_xhSQGKxO4

A WINGSUIT AND A PRAYER

**Take a helmet-cam flight through the narrowest
of crevices with The Flying Cowboy**

Just flying like an eagle in his wingsuit isn't enough for
adrenaline junkie Marshall Miller. The man they call the
"flying cowboy" was after a bigger buzz. He ventured to the
Vermillion Cliffs near Minneapolis, USA. There he leaps out of
a helicopter, takes flight and heads along the Beehive Line,
the narrowest of canyons. Like a real-life batman, he plunges
through a rocky gap in which he can almost reach out and
touch the sides. As Miller himself says on completing the
flight: "That was pretty cool, eh?"

http://y2u.be/ev5JqIJvbiE

TOILET ROLL TUTORIAL

Hilarious dad's tutorial for teenagers that goes heavy on the sarcasm

Tutorials are one of the great things about YouTube. You can learn anything from changing a carburettor to making a soufflé. This tutorial, heavily laced with irony, is one of the funniest. The father of two teenagers, tired of finding they wouldn't listen to him, resorted to making a YouTube video. He produced a step-by-step guide to removing a used roll of toilet paper and replacing it with a full one. He adds that an advanced level would involve putting the empty toilet roll in the bin, but admits that may be "a step too far at the moment".

http://y2u.be/pNOY2EZuvTU

SELFIE PROPOSAL

Awesome reaction to boyfriend who proposes while pretending to take a selfie

---

"Wha.. Oh Oh my God. Yeah. Are you serious right now? Is this for real? Oh My God, Oh my God! Yeeah!" YouTube does romance in the best possible way in this short video of a marriage proposal and the magnificent reaction it elicits. Lisa Holloway thought she was posing for a selfie, but it was really her boyfriend's sneaky way of filming his proposal. As he gets down on his knees and pulls out the ring, the camera catches her hilarious and touching, eye-stretching look and her words of total astonishment.

http://y2u.be/uH_Qu4ohdY0

3D? YOU BET!

**Check out this awesome 3D video installation
above a bar in a Vegas casino**

The competition to entice gamblers into their rooms has led
to some incredible displays in casinos. This video features an
amazing feature at the SLS Hotel in Las Vegas, where those trying
their luck are watched over by a giant three-dimensional golden
face peering down on the casino floor. The incredible display is
not a moving physical creation but a very clever optical illusion.
The LED-laden structure measuring 9.75 metres (32 feet) long
by 5.5 metres (18 feet) wide, and extending 1.2 metres (4 feet)
deep, uses 2.1 million multicoloured LEDs. Its pixels are spaced
at 6 millimetres (less than ¼ inch) to create a three-dimensional
appearance when viewed from beneath.

http://y2u.be/EWvQ0cgQwXQ

THE CAT THAT DOESN'T GIVE A...

You can plead and beg as much as you want, but this cat is just BAD

The title of this video, *Gato malo*, translates as "Bad Cat", but this cold-hearted moggie is something else. He certainly doesn't look like he'll be curling up with you on the sofa any time soon. He's a real Bond villain of a cat; a pure evil pedigree gangster. OK, it's really just a 35-second clip of a cat knocking things off a coffee table – but it's the look he gives, the way he pauses to listen to his owner's heartfelt pleas to stop before continuing anyway and his pure "couldn't give a damn" attitude that makes it a winner.

http://y2u.be/UoUEQYjYgf4

SHAKE A TAIL FEATHER

Has she gone? Right, it's time for this owl to throw some shapes

It's funny how some people just have to see a camera to start performing, while others are happy to ignore a photo opportunity. Well, this video proves that owls are no different. Wildlife photographer Megan Lorenz has a GoPro camera on her lawn filming a pair of burrowing owls. She has hardly got in the car to leave when the owls appear to start a dance-off, mugging it up in front of the camera. While one doesn't seem that bothered, the other is ready to pull some shapes and strut its stuff on the lawn.

http://y2u.be/SILvPVVAhBo

A MAN'S BEST FRIEND IS HIS ROBODOG

Introducing Spot, the electric-powered robot dog

You may have already seen BigDog, a gas-powered robot dog from the Boston Dynamic company. Now he has a little friend named Spot, who is electric-powered with a sensor head and super hydraulics. The 70-kilogram (160-pound) robot dog isn't the cutest mutt you've ever come across, but it can canter along next to a human, climb stairs and walk off-road. It can keep its balance when the meanest of people take a kick at it and most impressively, it can walk next to BigDog without succumbing to the urge to sniff its bottom.

http://y2u.be/M8YjvHYbZ9w

PERFECT PLAYMATES

A heartwarming montage of surprising animal friendships

Warning. This video montage is so full of cute images it could send you into an ahhhhhh overload. This ad for Android software shows a succession of the most unlikely combinations of animals surprisingly getting along like BFFs. There are elephants and dogs, monkeys and horses, and even dogs and cats all playing together and pulling at your heartstrings. Now, it is unashamed sentimentality, but who doesn't want to watch a tiger nuzzling up to a bear? A rodent taking a ride on a tortoise's back? Or a cat opening a door for a dog?

http://y2u.be/vnVuqfXohxc

FORWARD TO THE PAST

Skateboard hero Tony Hawks get first go on a futuristic Hoverboard

This is so cool. The 1989 film *Back To the Future Part II* finds Marty McFly (Michael J Fox) and his friend Emmett "Doc" Brown (Christopher Lloyd) travelling to the year 2015, where among other technological advances, they see people flying hoverboards. How fitting, then, that Lloyd is present when skateboard whizz Tony Hawks and other luminaries get to be the first to ride – or fly – this gravity-defying piece of wood for real. If you want more information, look up *Tony Hawk Has Something To Say About The New Hoverboard*.

http://y2u.be/08pSoZMUT10

COLA COOK-UP

You'll never drink cola again when you see what it boils down to...

Not much is known about the CrazyRussianHacker except he has a fabulous 007-style Russian accent and a range of cool experiments. Here, he tries boiling a bottle of cola to reveal just what you are putting in your body along with the carbonated water. The result is shocking – a huge dollop of sugar and chemicals – looking even worse when he's burnt it to kingdom come! The CrazyRussianHacker also has some neat life hacks: check out his potato peeling with an electric drill or how to open a can without a tin opener.

http://y2u.be/LZp29Qeu8_U

CLIMBING NIAGARA

Climbing up a frozen Niagra Falls for the first ever time

The Niagara Falls are the world's largest flowing waterfalls. People have gone over in barrels and tightrope walked across, but until January 2015, no one had ever climbed up the falls. *National Geographic*'s 2015 Adventurer of the Year, Will Gadd, took advantage of the falls icing up to scale the frozen sections up to the top along the line that separates Canada and the USA. In a little over an hour, Will and his assistant, Sarah Hueniken, climbed the 45 metres (150 feet), venturing close to the falling water and even to the ice behind the falls themselves.

http://y2u.be/jU5i1WjRBhE

TAKE A BOW

Mind-blowing archery from a man who has re-discovered ancient shooting skills

Lars Andersen has been called "The Clint Eastwood of Archery". Forget the bow and arrow merchants of *Lord of the Rings* or *Robin Hood*, Anderson's archery skill is completely different — and awesome. The Dane studied the forgotten techniques of ancient master archers and as a result is a world record holder in rapid fire archery. His video is an astonishing mash-up of history lesson and stunt action, which sees him de-bunk Hollywood myths and pull off stunts like shooting three arrows in a second with pinpoint accuracy, shooting an in-flight arrow, or catching and returning an incoming arrow.

http://y2u.be/BEG-ly9tQGk

EYE PLAY THE PIANO

**An astonishing virtual reality piano that
is played with the blink of an eye**

The "universal piano" is a unique and amazing use of Virtual
Reality technology. Through wearing a special VR headset,
a user can select single notes or chords on the piano with a
pointed gaze and through just a blink of the eye they can play
them. Even the piano's soft pedal effect can be invoked with
just a slight tilt of the head. It is, of course, a brilliant way of
enabling those with physical disabilities to play the piano, but
also opens up a world of new opportunites in the future.

http://y2u.be/VHXx7XTPULE

TEE TIME

**After an eight-year wait, Rory McIlroy
finally sinks a hole in one**

It has been achieved by amateurs, US Presidents, even Justin
Timberlake, but in all his games since turning professional in
2007, Northern Irishman Rory McIlroy had never enjoyed the
glory of a hole-in-one. He says he first sank an ace at the age of
nine and had holed a few first time in practice, but through all
his great tournament victories the holy grail of golf had eluded
him. Then he reached the tee at the 177-yard (162-metre),
par three fifteenth hole in the 2015 Abu Dhabi HSBC Golf
Championship. There his nine-iron shot bounced twice
before spinning into the cup.

http://y2u.be/Qy5YMVghzDY

NO ORDINARY JOE

**Impressive impressions from Joe Sugg,
the boy wonder of YouTube**

You are probably already aware of the ThatcherJoe channel, or at
least of its star performer, Joe Sugg. Zany, eccentric and good-
looking, the boyish 23-year-old has over three million subscribers
to his channel and a legion of fans he calls the Sugglets. One
of the biggest new stars of YouTube, Joe produces short videos
of challenges, pranks and impressions. This video is a good
example of his work. He's a pretty good impressionist with his
Elmo, Kermit, Shrek, Donkey and others being spot-on, but you'll
be won over by his charm, charisma and energy.

http://y2u.be/w42j-QWEqgY

FARTING ARCHY

**When Archy the horse lets rip, stand well back.
He really lets rip**

They say it's better out than in. And it's pretty obvious that's a
sentiment that this horse will agree with. Yes, this is a farting
video and a good one too – so if watching a horse fart itself
into ecstasy isn't your cup of tea, then move on, there's nothing
more to see here. This horse's name is Archy and the poor thing
has an intestinal issue that makes it difficult for him to pass
wind. So, he lies on his back, has a bit of a wriggle and
lets it all out in one long, marvellous fart.

http://y2u.be/jMyL0HdXPuc

PIRANHA FRENZY

Best not to dangle your big toe in this pool!

Those supposed scary films where people are fed to hungry piranhas are rubbish, aren't they? Well, take a look at this footage shot in a river in Brazil. Here a seemingly tranquil river is suddenly turned into a bubbling bloodbath as someone decides to drop a piece of meat into a pool of the sharp-jawed little terrors. Apparently, piranhas do actually feed in a frenzy. They attack by literally taking a bite out of their victim, stripping an animal of its flesh within a matter of minutes and even taking bites out of each other in their mad haste.

http://y2u.be/9qf1Uew_HVs

CELLO WARS

The Piano Guys fight an exciting lightsaber duel – on cellos!

Originally posting YouTube videos in order to advertise a piano shop in Utah, USA, The Piano Guys struck a chord (sorry!) with thousands of viewers. Armed with a cello and a piano, the Guys say that their aim is to put a new spin on classic music and a classic spin on new music. By October 2014, The Piano Guys' YouTube channel had more than half a billion total video views and a handful of viral videos. This is one of the most fun – a *Star Wars* medley played by a Jedi Master and a Sith Lord with appearances from Darth Vader and Chewbacca.

http://y2u.be/BgAlQuqzl8o

IN THE DOGHOUSE – AGAIN

Denver the Guilty Dog is back in a Christmas confessional

Remember Denver the Guilty Dog who was shamefacedly caught having devoured a bag of cat treats? If you haven't seen it, it's on the suggestion panel on the right. If you have, you are bound to remember the yellow Labrador and be delighted to find her in trouble again. This time Denver – in collaboration with the cat – has been feeding on the foam ornaments from the Christmas tree. The red dye around the dog's mouth is a dead giveaway, but poor Denver gives that look that says, "Okay you got me! I did it. I'm weak and naughty. Please, please forgive me." And who wouldn't?

http://y2u.be/ogZWYn6qHSk

HOT LAVA, COLD DRINK

Every wondered what happens when molten lava engulfs a cola can? Course you have...

This is just a short film of molten hot flowing lava slowly engulfing an unopened can of cola. No, don't skip it – it's strangely fascinating. Perhaps it is the juxtaposition of nature in its raw state and the most famous commercial object in the world; maybe it's the miraculous high definition of the GoPro camera that captures such incredible detail; or it could just be the hypnotic effect of watching to see what happens to the can. Whatever, I'm not the only one; the video has had 21 million views and counting.

http://y2u.be/GaSjwAu3yrI

SMART-HOUND BUS

It's a smart dog that knows it's own way to the park — by bus!

Passengers on a Seattle bus have grown used to seeing an unaccompanied dog taking up one of the seats. It roams the aisles looking for a spare seat, hops up and happily sits looking out the window. When the bus reaches the park, up he gets and waits for the doors to open. The owner of the dog is usually a bus or two behind, having waited to finish his cigarette. Eclipse is a black Labrador/bull mastiff cross and seems to charm all the passengers he meets on the bus.

http://y2u.be/Bz4XEpK6INU

TRUE ROMANCE

True romance as flower girl and ring bearer boy marry 20 years later

---

It was the love story of the year. When Americans Brittney and Briggs Fussy got married at St Paul, Minnesota, it wasn't the first time the couple had walked down the aisle together. In 1995, she had been the flower girl and he was the ring bearer at a wedding between their families — they had walked to the front of the church arm in arm. Fifteen years later, she recognizes him in class and a romance blossoms. Fast forward another five years, and there they are dressed in their finery again — and this time they are the main act.

http://y2u.be/edVau9m6vHI

SHEET CHEAT

**You didn't know you didn't know, but
you'll be glad you know now...**

"One of the biggest challenges you're going to face in life,"
begins Jill Cooper from LivingOnADime.com, "is how to fold a
fitted sheet." One wonders what kind of charmed life Jill has
led? Don't worry, it gets better. In fact, more than ten million
people have viewed this helpful and practical video on sheet
folding – and the comments prove it is undoubtedly a useful
tip. The video itself is also proof of the fount of knowledge
shared on YouTube, where you can find a tutorial on
almost all of life's challenges.

http://y2u.be/_Z5k9nWcuFc

BEAUTY FROM CHAOS

**Mousetraps and ping pong balls create
an explosive New Year celebration**

Stealing an idea from a science experiment on the chain reaction of nuclear physics, this incredible Pepsi stunt proves nothing except how beautiful ordered chaos can be. To celebrate the 2015 New Year, 2,014 mousetraps were armed and loaded with 2,015 Ping-Pong balls (eagle-eyed pedants might spot the advertising exaggeration, there are actually 1650 mousetraps and 1840 ping-pong balls). Triggered, by a single ball, the result is a brilliant spectacle of flying balls and cartwheeling traps. The whole stunt took five hours to set up and took just 15 seconds from the first flying ball to the explosive conclusion.

http://y2u.be/-zX-gz1lRt0

BLINDFOLD LIMBO

Limbo dancing – without the bar. It's very funny

If you like a simple practical joke, you might just enjoy this clip from a humorous Norwegian TV show, set in Karl Johan's Gate in the centre of Oslo. The set-up here is brilliantly simple. After getting unsuspecting passers-by and shoppers to have a go at limbo dancing under a stick, the pranksters then suggest they try limboing while wearing a blindfold. As the foil begins leaning backwards, the duo disappear up the street with the bar. Who would guess that watching someone walking along while bent over backwards wearing a blindfold could be quite so amusing?

http://y2u.be/Vi41zAu4FfM

POOR GUMMY

How many times can a man shoot a giant gummy bear in the name of science?

This is a scientific experiment that is difficult to explain – or justify. This guy has taken a particular dislike to a gummy bear. Maybe it was that really, really irritating song that was a massive hit on YouTube. So, he takes a giant "world's largest" gummy bear and shoots it with a .22 rifle. Then he shoots it with a 12 gauge shotgun. Poor Gummy has a hole through him and part of his back missing, but the sadist then freezes him by submerging him in liquid nitrogen and repeats the 12 gauge test. Gummy doesn't come out of it well.

http://y2u.be/R2H0ZhO1NWl

HEART-WARMING HANDOUT

**A homeless man is given $100 in cash.
How will he spend it?**

This video by YouTube prankster Josh Paler Lin kicked up a real
storm when it went viral around Christmas 2014. In it we see
Paler Lin giving $100 in cash to a random homeless man. He
then follows him with a hidden camera to see just how he spends
the money. As Paler Lin and many others guessed, the man heads
straight for a liquor (alcohol) store, but it was what happened
next that both surprised and shocked. The story found its way
to TV news bulletins around the world, but also found some
claiming the whole thing was staged.

http://y2u.be/AUBTAdl7zuY

ONCE MORE FROM THE TOP

BASE jumping from the highest skyscraper in the world

The Khalifa Tower (Burj Hkalifa), a skyscraper in Dubai, is the highest man-made structure in the world. It stands to reason that someone would jump off it. BASE jumpers Fred Fugen and Vince Reffet set a world record in 2014 when they leapt from a platform built above the top of the building, some 828 metres (2,716 feet 6 inches) from the ground. To make sure the video was impressive, they actually did the jump six times – in both free-fly mode and wingsuits – and circled the building one and a quarter times on the way down.

http://y2u.be/iD4qsWnjsNU

CHANGING BATTERIES

A sad but wonderful five-minute animation

YouTube is home to a fabulous collection of short films, especially animations. There are so many five- or ten-minute perfectly told stories that will make you laugh or cry and often both. This short film, *Changing Batteries*, has been around for a year or so, but keeps finding new viewers as people rave about it online. It tells the moving story of the relationship between an old lady and a robot. A word of warning, though: if you are easily moved to tears, it might be worth having a box of tissues nearby.

http://y2u.be/O_yVo3YOfqQ

CAMERON'S CONFERENCE RAP

Marvellous mash-up puts the Prime Minister on the mic

This video contains a rude word or two (not many), but if you can live with that it's very funny indeed. Michael Bollen and Steve Warlin, who together comprise Cassetteboy, have form. They were responsible for the wicked (in both senses!) *Nick Clegg says I'm Sorry* video and a series of other classic mash-ups. Using Enimen's 'Lose Yourself' as a backing track, they brilliantly edit together a series of rhymes such as "I'm not saying it's not funny / It is for me, I've got loads of money" and somehow emerge with a coherent song. Ace work.

http://y2u.be/0YBumQHPAeU

RAPPING RADCLIFFE

Harry Potter star displays his rapping skills – and he nails it!

He's no longer Harry Potter, but actor Daniel Radcliffe still carries a touch of magic about him wherever he goes. Here he is on *The Tonight Show* in the US telling host Jimmy Fallon that he was inspired by Enimen and "had kind of an obsession with memorizing complicated, lyrically intricate and fast songs." We knew what was coming next... Daniel stood up and performed a word perfect rendition of Blackalicious' 'Alphabet Aerobics'. If you are looking for more evidence of Mr Radcliffe's verbal dexterity you could look up his performance of 'The Elements Song' on *The Graham Norton Show*.

http://y2u.be/aKdV5FvXLuI

MOUTHFUL OF SAUCE

Italian-American chef finds "Worcestershire Sauce" a real mouthful

Pasquale Sciarappa's shirt may say, "No Sweat, No Sauce", but he manages to work up quite a sweat over his pronunciation of a certain British condiment. The 75-year-old Italian-American chef has been uploading his recipe videos to YouTube since 2008, but none have gone as viral as his charming attempts to pronounce the classic Worcestershire Sauce. His recipe for Stuffed Mushrooms required a dash of the sauce, but when he came to naming the special ingredient he faltered. Always a difficult word for a non-English speaker, Pasquale struggles to get his tongue around "Worcestershire" for over a minute before giving up.

http://y2u.be/YwTT8YQFJDQ

YOU'VE GOT TO BE JOKING

Record-breaking comedian fires off 32 jokes in a minute

"Went to buy a telescope... They saw me coming!", "Pollen count – that's a tough job!". OK, they may not all be funny, but you will surely laugh at one of Clive Greenaway's jokes. After all, he rattled off 32 of them in a minute. The professional Tommy Cooper impersonator officially broke the world record with 26 jokes at a show at in Suffolk, meeting the Guinness Records qualification of having a live audience and getting a reaction (if not a laugh) with every joke. The next evening he went on the BBC's *Newsnight* programme to better his effort – unofficially.

http://y2u.be/QF2JaMnLm-4

BOHEMIAN CARSODY

**Aussie beauties send YouTube wild
with in-car Queen singalong**

Recreating the famous *Wayne's World* in-car singalong to
Queen's hit 'Bohemian Rhapsody" has been a long time meme
on YouTube. But Australian female comedy trio SketchShe
really nail it in this 2015 video. Sydney actresses Lana Kington,
Madison Lloyd and Shae-Lee Shackleford throw themselves into
the song in a tight performance full of humour (catch the cheesy
literal mimes), flirtatiousness and energy. Their good looks and
impressive lip-synching helped them racked up 17 million views
in its first two weeks — a good effort but still a long way behind
Queen's original; that has 130 million views!

http://y2u.be/aVx6cXf5Liw

JURASS-BRICK PARK

Great version of *Jurassic Park* with humour, authenticity and LEGO bricks

A father and his eight-year-old daughter put together this excellent three-minute LEGO version of the dinosaur film *Jurassic Park*. The stop-motion film recreates some and scary moments – including the attack of the velociraptors at the museum – just using LEGO bricks. OK, it helps that dad Paul Hollingsworth is a film editor and animation director with access to $100,000 worth of LEGO bricks and a small team of animation industry professionals, but daughter Hailee makes sure it keeps its homemade charm and naive appeal.

http://y2u.be/5KNMYi5MDhE

DOMINO HOUSE PARTY

**A video which takes the falling domino theme
and goes somewhere very magical**

I can understand if you see the word "dominoes" and think
"Maybe I'll skip this one", but this is pretty jaw-dropping. First
of all, it's a video to a cracking tune in A-Trak and Tommy Trash's
'Tuna Melt' and secondly, it isn't a domino fall but a domino-
effect kinetic sculpture – so there! OK, there are dominoes, but
these critters climb staircases, turn on taps and unleash pool
balls, set off a feather-scattering fan and explode stick bombs.
And, they kick off a marvellous multi-coloured tour through
the rooms of a two-story house using collapsing toast, a paper
airplane, an unravelling necklace and an underwater submarine.

http://youtu.be/T8b-2biI8wU

CANINE CUDDLE

**A distressed dog is comforted by his
canine pal in this feelgood clip**

What would be happening in a dog's nightmare? Do they
dream of zombie dogs on the rampage? Failing their test at
the obedience class? Or something as simple as the family
getting a new cat? Jackson, a pretty wonderful-looking,
one-year-old "Double Doodle" (the poster says that's half
goldendoodle and half labradoodle) is having a bad dream
involving a lot of scurrying actions. Fortunately, help is at
hand in the form of his canine friend Laika. His reaction to
his young pal's discomfort is heart-warming. As one comment
says, we all need a Laika in our lives.

http://y2u.be/uTy_wUkWpkM

CLASSIC INTERPRETATION

Simply brilliant funky sign language interpretation of Swedish Eurovision song

Magnus Carlsson's attempt to represent Sweden at the Eurovision Song Contest in 2015 fell a little flat when his up tempo song was voted ninth out of 12 entries. His song, however, was the talk of the nation thanks to the performance of the sign language interpreter, Tommy Krångh. Tommy's interpretation of the song didn't just communicate the lyrics to the hard of hearing, he communicated the feel of the song too. "I get funky and just let go," the 48-year-old told Swedish newspaper *Aftonbladet* after becoming an overnight sensation. There are now calls for Tommy to interpret for Måns Zelmerlöw, Sweden's winning entry for Eurovision.

http://y2u.be/S00eBrQBPNc

LAMBORGHINI AVINGACRASH

**One of the world's most expensive cars goes
out of control on a London street**

If you owned a rare Lamborghini Aventador worth around
£300,000, would you risk it on the busy streets of London? The
700-horsepower Aventador is capable of accelerating from a
standstill to over 96km/h (60mph) in just 2.9 seconds. That can
be pretty useful on a racetrack, but is just asking for trouble
in the city's rush hour where a potential prang is always just
around the corner. So, to upmarket West London, where
the owner of this matt black Aventador decides to put
his foot down on a quiet stretch of road...

http://y2u.be/kfS8iz2NaLE

NATURE'S LIGHT SHOW

Incredible time-lapse film of the Northern Lights

This beautiful time-lapse sequence was made by filmmaker Alexis Coram using 3,500 images shot over three nights in Alaska. The Northern Lights (scientific name: aurora borealis) are nature's own spectacular light show. The beautifully coloured lights that illuminate the sky are the result of collisions between electrically charged particles from the sun as they enter the earth's atmosphere. Carefully edited to a great soundtrack, Coram's breathtaking film shows the phenomenon in all its glory, bringing out not only the wonderful greens, yellows and pinks but also the fascinating movement of the lights.

http://y2u.be/x7M-uXMBjwg

HEY, OBAMA – WHY DON'T YOU JUST...

President Obama reads some of the mean things said about him on Twitter

---

Say what you like about American President Obama, but the guy certainly does have a sense of humour. A US chat show, *Jimmy Kimmel Live!*, has been running a series of films of celebrities reading aloud some of the nasty things said about them on Twitter. Hollywood's great and good have all appeared (they are generally very funny and available to view on YouTube), but few would have expected the most powerful man on Earth to join in the self-ribbing. Some are funny, some are mean, but the President takes them all in the best humour.

http://y2u.be/RDocnbkHjhl

BIG SISTER REVELATION

A little girl's surprise reaction to the news that she's going to be a big sister

It's a big moment for Dad. He's got to tell his three-year-old daughter, Kathryn, that she is soon to become a big sister. It's a stressful moment for a young child, so dad's prepared well. He's sat her down, he's bought her a book to help things along and he's got the camera rolling to record the moment for posterity. "You know why we got you this?" he asks her, pointing to the book. Then he unleashes the big news: "You're going to be a big sister!" No one, but no one could predict what happens next...

http://y2u.be/3ltFHI2c7-s

GAMER GRANNY GOES BALLISTIC!

Overexcited Granny gets revenge on British Gas on Grand Theft Auto

She uses some pretty foul language, but most people were able to excuse this granny as she gets immersed in a game of *Grand Theft Auto*. The senior citizen had just received an inflated gas bill from British Gas and used the game to vent her anger at the fuel suppliers. Off she goes on a hilarious killing spree of imaginary British Gas executives, shouting "Die, die, die" and swearing like a sailor as she blasts away with a sub-machine gun. I just hope she's calmed down by time the guy comes to read the meter.

http://y2u.be/HT3nrP4U6Nw

WET WEDDING

The best wedding video ever sees the whole party fall in a lake

Dan and Jackie Anderson really splashed out for their wedding in Minnesota, USA. When the family and close friends joined them for some photos before the wedding, the bride and groom discovered they weren't the only ones taking the plunge. As the 22-strong party lined up on a wooden dock, the structure gave way beneath their weight. A few bridesmaids managed to escape, but everyone else ended up submerged in the water. After collecting some unique wedding snaps, they had a quick towel down and the ceremony went ahead as planned.

http://y2u.be/UaXaSfHuFu8

MELTING MOMENT

First-hand footage of the collapse of a massive iceberg arch

Wanda Stead and her husband's lovely boat trip out on the Bay of Exploits in Newfoundland was interrupted by the sudden collapse of an iceberg in the bay. Wanda was left fearing for her life as the arch in the iceberg suddenly started to crack, and within seconds, tons of ice began falling into the waters below. Wanda's video footage captures the dramatic disintegration of the iceberg, but also the panic as the large waves formed started to approach their boat. She sounds pretty terrified as she shouts to her husband, "Run, Rick, go — go!"

http://y2u.be/XEk5mNVc2Hk

DINNER FOR ONE... HAMSTER

A hamster eating tiny burritos – it's what YouTube was made for!

YouTube comedy group HelloDenizen combined two of the sites current favourites – miniature food and small rodents – and earned themselves a viral hit. Chef Farley Elliott meticulously chops vegetables and rolls them into tiny flour tortillas. He then takes his freshly prepared burritos over to the smallest of tables set up in a miniature restaurant. It's now dinner time for his little hamster friend who, to the chef's great relief, tucks into his haute cuisine fair with gusto. And that's it. That's how you create a video that's been viewed 10 million times!

http://y2u.be/JOCtdw9FG-s

TERMINAL BLUES

How bored do you have to be to lip-sync Celine Dion?

"What do you do when you are stuck at the Las Vegas Airport overnight?" asks Richard Dunn at the beginning of this video. His answer: "Shoot a music video on your iPhone. That's what." Instead of wallowing in his hopeless situation, Dunn filmed himself lip-syncing Celine Dion's 'All By Myself' in various heart-rending situations around the airport – from outside the women's toilets to the check in desks to the x-ray tables. It is an hilarious night's work and we can be thankful that for once what happened in Vegas didn't stay in Vegas.

http://y2u.be/m81-SVgHUCs

DANCING DIVA

The moment Brendan Jordan, the dancing diva, found the spotlight

---

"Every time I see a spotlight," 15-year-old Brendan Jordan said on TV, "there's this mode I snap into, and my inner superstar comes out!" Back in October 2014, Brendan was just another face in the crowd as a local television reporter covered the opening of a shopping mall in Las Vegas. Having elbowed his way to the front of the crowd, Brendan began to preen, pose, vogue and completely photobomb the shoot. America took the dancing diva to their hearts, as he was feted on chat shows, became an American Apparel model and an ambassador for an LGBT anti-bullying campaign.

http://y2u.be/yOOyfymbipg

RUSSIAN COFFEE

**In the midst of violence and chaos, one man
sits and sips his coffee**

Every now and then, something crops up on YouTube which is
intriguing, baffling and beyond explanation. This clip is titled
Just another day in Russia and has around seven million views.
It shows a terrifying moment when around 40 thugs, many of
them masked and some possibly armed, storm a restaurant.
They obviously target some customers, while others slip away as
quickly as possible – except for one man. As all hell breaks loose
around him, this one man sits quietly in the middle of the fracas
and casually sips his coffee. It is all quite bizarre.

http://y2u.be/lmpLZalaaGU

A REAL BUZZ

Does this bumble bee really give a guy a high five?

Amid the pop videos, corporate ads and professional pranksters, there is still room on YouTube for the casual amateur to post something special. Now, you might not consider this footage of a bumble bee giving what is perceived to be a high five to a young man as special, but it has been viewed a one-and-a-half million times with over 8,000 thumbs up. While some killjoys have suggested that the bee is actually making a "back off" gesture, I'd prefer to think that the man's clear high spirits have won over an insect better known for its belligerence.

http://y2u.be/AgU4gXgIEsg

CHANDELIER RE-IMAGINED

Losing bet man reproduces Sia's viral video in his own apartment

The music video for Sia's single 'Chandelier' was one of the biggest YouTube hits of 2014. It featured 11-year-old dancer Maddie Ziegler, who spins, kicks, twirls and leaps around in a deserted apartment. The video was nominated for a Grammy and received considerable critical acclaim. In less than a year it has been viewed a phenomenal 600 million times and unsurprisingly, it has inspired many parodies, including one by Hollywood star Jim Carey. This, however, is my favourite. Apparently made as the result of losing a football bet, the video shows Chuck Jose copying the moves shot for shot in his own apartment.

http://y2u.be/5v24i9XTJq0

A ROARING SUCCESS

Getting a hug from a fully grown lion

Conservationist Valentin Gruener rescued Sirga, a lion cub, after she was driven out of her pride. Alone in the desert plains of Botswana, Africa, she would have faced certain death. He nursed her back to health and took her in to the Modisa Wildlife Project. Three years later, Sirga is still at the project and is learning to hunt for prey on her own in the hope to return her to the wild. She is now a fully grown 50-kilogram (110-pound) lioness, but as this amazing clip shows she still recognizes and shows incredible affection for the man who saved her life.

http://y2u.be/a4dWTKo5u7M

MIGHTY MOUTH

Big Mouth strikes again – and again

"Big Mouth" is usually a term of abuse, but for 20-year-old Francisco Domingo Joaquim, aka Chiquinho, from Angola it is the greatest accolade. For the man nicknamed "The Angolan Jaw of Awe" really does have the biggest mouth in the world. His elastic lips and mouth have been measured at 17 centimetres (6.69 inches) at full gape. From performing at the local market, he is now appearing around the world. On a recent Italian TV show, he amazed the audience by placing and removing a can of cola from his mouth 14 times in under a minute.

http://y2u.be/NO3C2s8rhBQ

MAN'S BEST FRIEND

Dog to the rescue in not near-drowning accident

This dog is never off duty. Despite reclining on the river bank, he's got an eye on his human friend who is having a dip on the river. And the watchful canine fears the worst when he sees the swimmer's head dip underwater. He jumps straight into the river and lands right on his owner's head. He's not finished yet. Grabbing the man's hand in his mouth he starts paddling away and pulling him back to shore. Although the swimmer was fine all along — it was reassuring to know his best pal was looking out for him.

http://y2u.be/dSF8B45AcDw

CREEPIEST MEAL EVER

Would you like to see the food on your plate come back to life?

Like the squid on the plate, this video just won't die – going viral again and again. Called "the creepiest meal ever", it shows a cuttlefish apparently coming back to life after being showered with soy sauce. The dish, a favourite in Japan, is called *Odori don*, which literally means "dancing rice squid bowl". Of course, the headless creature is not really coming back to life – it is just the salt in the sauce reacting with the still fresh squid's nerve ends. Nevertheless, it's the kind of thing that could put you off your dinner.

http://y2u.be/dxQmOR_QLfQ

RUN, RUN – IT'S AN ANGRY TORTOISE!

An explorer and a tortoise in the slowest chase scene ever

When an explorer on Assumption Island in the Indian Ocean, interrupts a pair of mating giant tortoises, the male is not happy. After his mate gives him a quick peck on the cheek and hides modestly in the bushes, the shell-shocked tortoise goes on the warpath. What ensues is the slowest chase seen ever, with the tortoise plodding insistently after the explorer. Meanwhile, we are hoping the creature puts on a sudden turn of speed, or leaps through the air to bring the interloper down. Wildlife footage with entertainment value – this is what we want!

http://y2u.be/RjtCS0EEoCY